THE WORLD FOLKTALE LIBRARY

Tales from Ancient Greece

Tales from Ancient Greece

By Frederick J. Moffitt

Illustrated by Bill Shields

Consultants

Moritz A. Jagendorf
Author and Folklorist

Carolyn W. Field
Coordinator of Work with Children
The Free Library of Philadelphia

SILVER BURDETT COMPANY

Morristown, New Jersey
Glenview, Ill. • Palo Alto • Dallas • Atlanta

INTRODUCTION

Folktales are old and fun to listen to. They may come from unfamiliar people and different parts of the world, but there is something in each one that you will recognize and understand. Most folktales are stories that were told and retold long before the invention of books and printing. That is how they got their name. They were passed along by word of mouth—one folk told another folk. Parents told their children. Neighbor shared with neighbor. Village folk told stories to entertain guests and travelers, who carried them to other parts of the world.

Folktales are not usually about real people or actual events, but in a way they are almost always true. They tell us something real about the people who make them up and pass them along. Folktales express the values of a society and reveal that society's ideas about living and surviving.

Many of the people and events in these tales from ancient Greece are based on history. The Trojan War that you will read about was actually fought. But it may not have happened as described in the legend. The story of Odysseus may tell about parts of the lives of many heroes of his day. "A Story Is Born" explains some of the details.   THE EDITOR

Library of Congress Catalog Card Number: 78-56059

CONTENTS

A STORY IS BORN

Over three thousand years ago, a fleet of Greek warships sailed for Troy. Helen, the queen of a Greek kingdom, had been kidnapped by Paris, a prince of Troy. Troy was a city kingdom in Asia Minor. The kidnapping began a war that lasted nearly ten years.

The warrior king Odysseus ruled Ithaca, a tiny Greek island off the mainland. When the war began, he left his kingdom and his family to join the Greek armies that were going to rescue Helen.

The rich city of Troy was surrounded by a huge limestone wall that kept the Greeks from entering the fortress.

Odysseus made a clever plan to capture the city. The Greeks built a huge wooden horse that was hollow inside. They left it outside the gates of the city and pretended to leave the shores of Troy. A prophet had warned the Trojans about gifts from the Greeks. The Trojans were curious anyway. Sinon, a Greek in disguise, explained to the Trojans that the Horse had been built by the Greeks as a peace offering to Athene. Believing the war had ended, the Trojans took the huge Horse into their city. While they slept, Sinon opened a secret door in the belly of the Horse and released the Greek soldiers who were hiding inside. They lit a torch to signal the Greek ships, which were waiting offshore. When the fighting was over, the city of Troy was left in smoldering ruins.

The story of the Trojan War is told in the *Iliad*, one of the oldest epic poems. It was probably first passed by word of mouth like most legends. Several hundred years later, the Greek poet Homer wrote it down.

Homer wrote another great epic poem called the *Odyssey*. It begins where the *Iliad* ends. The *Odyssey* describes the return voyage of Odysseus from Troy to his kingdom, Ithaca.

The gods and goddesses of Greek mythology play important roles in the *Iliad* and the *Odyssey*. The goddess Athene was on the side of the Greeks. She had used her supernatural powers to help the Greeks defeat the Trojans. At the war's end, some of the Greeks became greedy. They looted the temple of Athene in Troy. To avenge this outrage, Athene asked Zeus to punish the Greeks. This explains the savage storms and many misfortunes that plagued Odysseus throughout his voyage home. After Odysseus had wandered for ten years over the seas surrounding the Greek islands, Athene took pity on him. She asked that Zeus allow Odysseus to return to Ithaca.

The "Diary" and "The Eagle and the Geese" are based on Homer's *Odyssey*. The "Diary" tells the story of the harrowing experiences of the voyage. "The Eagle and the Geese" tells of the terrible situation that awaited Odysseus when he arrived in Ithaca ten years later.

The "Diary" of Odysseus begins a week after the Greeks have left Troy. With six hundred Greek soldiers, he has stopped to collect treasures and provisions from the city of Ismanus. It was a matter of pride for Greek warriors to return home with ships loaded with treasure.

DIARY

We made good speed from Troy, the winds being favorable. Food and water lasts no time at all for the 50 or so men on each of the 12 ships in my fleet. So when we arrived near Ismarus, the land of the Cicones, we decided to take on provisions. We sacked the city — stripped it of wealth and great quantities of food and wine for the voyage. We slaughtered the sheep and oxen on the shore. I told them, "Pack the provisions, and let's push on at once."

It was useless. My men are hardened by 10 years of savage war. Close quarters and inactivity have made them restless. These wolves of war had enjoyed the fury of fighting the Cicones and were now glutting themselves. They were in no mood to leave.

As I expected, there followed a fierce attack by the Cicones and their neighbors that lasted from dawn to sunset. They swept upon us like a swarm of bees. The battle was bloody and costly. We lost more than 72 men.

Twenty-ninth day: Moored near shore

That great captain of the clouds, Zeus, blinded our voyage by throwing clouds over land and sea. The howling squalls made ribbons of our sails and splinters of our masts. At last we rowed our ships to this island. I know not the direction we came or the name of this island. Zeus has made my navigation charts useless with his untiring storms. For two days we mended and repaired our ships. The weather favorable, we are now ready to cast off in this golden dawn. The new masts are stout, in spite of being sap green, and the sails blinding-white in the morning sun.

Second month, second week: Raging storms

At first the seas were calm and the winds steady. Had they lasted, I would now be in sight of Ithaca. Throughout this good weather, I was able to navigate and plot a course. But after Cape Maleia, we were sucked full force into the mouths of angry winds. Who knows how long we will be victims of Zeus' blasts!

Second month, third week: Lotus Land

The seas calmed on the tenth day, making possible navigation of the inlets. We landed on the beach to fill our water butts. I sent several men to scout the land and forage for food. Time passed, and they did not return. I set out with six of my crew to look for them. We found them surrounded by the Lotus-eaters, a gay, carefree people. I called out to the men, saying they must leave with us. But they had eaten the lotus fruit and were drugged by its sweet poison. They did not know their own names — they did not recognize me. I spoke of their homes and Ithaca. They were drugged and insensible.

Finally I ordered them dragged to the ships and put

in chains under the thwarts until the drug wore off. They cried out and struggled to get loose. Fearing that the other men would slip away and find their way to the Lotus-eaters, I fastened them to their benches. I told them to beat their oars with all speed. I felt safe only when we were well out of sight of Lotus Land.

Third month: Island of the Cyclopes

It must have been the gods who brought our ships safely to this plenteous and untilled island. Last night the thick fog blotted the other ships from sight. No beam from a heavenly body cracked through the low-hung clouds. We waited through the night for Aurora, Goddess of Dawn.

We woke to discover a beautiful harbor and, beyond, a lush and abundant island. With longbows and spears we went to the untouched, unexplored island to hunt animals that had never seen men before. That night each ship had 9 goats and mine had 10. We feasted and offered a sacrifice to Zeus, patron god of travelers in foreign lands. On the island across the bay, we could see smoke rising from the caves of the Cyclopes, and we could even hear their thunderous voices. Tired and contented, the men stretched out on the beach and were lulled to sleep by the sound of the long, unbroken waves rolling in on the shore.

I sit here occupied with thoughts of the Cyclopes. Curiosity urges me to seek them out and see what welcome a civilized man could win from these cannibals.

Fourth month, first week: The Cyclops' cave

This morning my crew and I went across the bay to the Cyclopes' island. We beached the ship at a distance from a cave, hidden in a shelter of poplars and craggy reefs. Addressing my crew, I spoke in this manner:

"A dozen of you will come with me to ask the meed of every traveler and to stake our claim for the guest-present. I am a man of subtle mind and endless resourcefulness. Ye gods, I shall exercise them to the fullest this day. The Cyclopes are one-eyed giants—cannibals and savages of enormous strength and size. The rest of you will stand by, alert to any emergency. You must be prepared to cast off in a churning foam of speed when we return."

With 12 of my bravest men and a butt skin of the rarest wine that was given me by the priest of Apollo in Ismarus, I entered the lair of the giant.

Lest my eye's memory fail me, I am sketching, however crudely, the plan and furnishings of this prosperous cave. In one corner are racks of cheeses. Nearby are wicker baskets in which cheese is made. Along the other side, the pens for the sheep and goats are partitioned in such a way ——

I am occupying myself with these sketches and notes while awaiting the Cyclops. He must be out in the pasture with his herds.

We meet the Cyclops

The Cyclopes are a proud and wicked race of giants who recognize no gods or laws. They rule themselves and live in caves on mountaintops. I knew no horror in war equal to the savagery of Polyphemus, the Cyclops, and son of Poseidon. I now set down the events of the most wicked and hair-raising episode in the entire three months of our voyage.

At sundown Polyphemus returned, driving his splendid herd and carrying an enormous quantity of wood for his fire. His burden was dropped with a reechoing crash

that sent my men flying into the corners of the cave. The deafening noise did not frighten them as much as did the giant's awful appearance.

The Cyclops looked like a jagged rock that juts from the side of a mountain. He drove the last of his herd into the cave, and then slipped a huge slab of stone over the opening. Ten yoke of oxen could not have budged that stone. We were trapped.

The clumsy oaf set about his household tasks, taking no notice of his uninvited guests. He milked his ewes and milch goats. He took the lambs and kids from their pens and placed them gently near their mothers for the night. He placed half the milk buckets in baskets for curd. And half he set aside for his food. I held my breath as he went near the cheese racks. My men and I had hungrily eaten a piece of the cheese and drunk some of the milk. As he moved closer, I felt certain that he would see what we had done. But the Cyclops continued to go heavily about his chores without noticing.

When he bent down to rebuild his fire, he turned toward me. The eye fixed in the center of his forehead was as large as a chariot wheel. It opened wide, and glared with the light of the fire. It was more stupid looking than frightening.

"Who are ye tha' dare enter th' cavern o' Polyphemus? Are ye pirates tha' thieve on th' seas?" he roared. His words sounded like the rushing of a waterfall.

I answered him politely. "In Zeus' name, provide us with shelter and food in this strange land."

"A Cyclops fears no god! Zeus is m' uncle an' I forge

his thunderbolts. Watch you don't cross me. I'm his favo-
rite Cyclops."

He craftily asked where our ship was. I answered
craft with craft, and told him we were shipwrecked and
had to swim ashore.

He then cast his lantern-eye glare on my men and flung
out both hands, seizing two of them. They sounded like
squealing swine at the slaughter. Before my eyes he
knocked them both senseless on the floor of the cave and
ate them. He drank some raw milk and stretched himself
on the floor and began to snore loudly. This bloodthirsty

savage will finish the rest of us, as he did my two brave men.

*   *   *

I have written this by the light of the fire, and my bones are still chilled by what I have seen tonight. We cannot escape. I would go for him this minute — I have my blade at my side — but for that stone that seals the cave. I am a prisoner, and can only dream of escaping.

The following day

This morning the monstrous idiot ate as he did the night before. He left with his herds and slipped the stone across the opening, shutting us in with the darkness.

Of my 12 men, 4 are gone. Who will it be tonight? Tomorrow? My teeth grind at these thoughts. Today we built a fierce fire and I spoke to my men. It took great courage, for we were all sick at heart. Together we planned to sharpen the butt of a green olive trunk with our blades and season it over the fire. Tonight we plan to drive it into his eye as he sleeps. Beyond this I cannot plan or even occupy myself with my notes. My men have already finished sharpening the trunk. I am stopping now, as my brains are seething to wipe out this fiend.

Third day: The deed is done

We are under way again. My men flail their oars, and the sea hisses as I record the events of the last day.

*   *   *

Last night the man-eater returned. He repeated the fare of his breakfast and did away with two more, making in all six brave men. Last night Antiphas, an expert with the spear, was cooked before being eaten!

This time I befriended the savage giant by offering the potent wine I had with me, saying we had managed to salvage it from the wreck. He gulped it down — the whole skin. He marveled at its flavor and spoke gleefully.

He asked my name. I answered that it was Nobody and suggested he do me a favor, since I had offered him the wine as a priceless host-gift. He promised to eat me last. There was no reasoning with this uncouth lout.

At last he tumbled on the ground and slept. We picked up the olive trunk and heated the pointed end over the fire until it was glowing red. I then took a position above the sleeping giant. Four of my men carried the huge trunk and raised it toward me. As they held it up, I drove it into his eye full force, twirling it several times,

and plunged it deep, as a shipbuilder drives his mast firmly into place.

A piercing roar cracked the cave and reechoed like thunder. The whelp's shrill screams flushed the bats from the ceiling of the cave and aroused the neighboring Cyclopes. They demanded to know why he woke them with such cries.

"Nobody ha' blinded me! Nobody's tryin' t' kill me! Roll 'way th' stone an' seize 'm," he bellowed.

"If nobody's botherin' ye, then Zeus must be punishing ye with nightmares. Why don't ye call your sire, King Poseidon, for help?" they grumbled.

His teeth clenched in agony, Polyphemus plucked the stake from his sizzling eye socket. His arms thrashed wildly about, trying to snatch one of us. I beckoned my men over to the sheep pens and picked 18 of the largest ewes. Using some hemp we found lying behind the pens, I bound these animals together in lots of three. Then I motioned to my men, and I bound them under the bellies of the richly fleeced beasts. Thus we spent the night, while the Cyclops lay against the slab door, moaning and crying out.

At dawn the flock got to its feet and trooped toward the door, which the giant had slid open during the night. His blind bulk blocked the arch to make certain none but the animals passed him. As they filed by, he cautiously felt them to be sure no one left astride the sheep. I hurled myself under his prize ram, my fists buried in his wool. He stopped his pet, holding one horn with his hairy hand.

"Why ha' ye wait so long? Did wan' t' stay wi' poor,

wounded Polyphemus?" he piteously growled into its ear.

My hands were wet with sweat—my grip was slipping. Finally he patted the sheep on the back and pushed it out. I was the last to leave the cave of horrors.

Once clear of the cave, I unloosed my men and we drove the sheep toward the galley. The victory over the Cyclops burst within me. When we had got aboard I shouted back, "Polyphemus, you have supped on your last Greek. We are free."

He loomed outside the cave and dashed about to catch us. But we had shipped oars and stood off a distance from the beach. In a rage, he tore off the top of the mountain and threw it, just missing our sweep. The sea swelled enormously, sending the ship flying back toward the shore.

My men turned on me, begging me to hold my tongue. They valued their lives and did not want any further dealings with Polyphemus. The crew desperately bent their backs to the oars. But I still could not restrain my words. When we had reached a safe distance I brashly boasted:

"Don't fail to say it was Odysseus, King of Ithaca and ravager of cities, who put out your eye."

Hearing my name, the Cyclops fell to his knees, saying that a prophet once told him Odysseus would one day put out his eye. But the prophet had described me as a man of great height and physical strength. For years Polyphemus watched for this godlike Odysseus to appear. He never expected Odysseus to be a pigmy. He then called upon his father, Poseidon, to wrap a belt of storms

about the earth to prevent my safe voyage home. Even if I should endure the storms, he said that I would arrive home, without crew or ship, to find great trouble in my palace.

Into the sixth month: Aeolus

It is now a month since we have been guests of King Aeolus, Guardian of the Winds. This splendid palace with its marble halls has made me homesick for my own home and kingdom.

I do not despair of the time spent here. It has been a boon to the spirits of my men, who have suffered many hardships. I have spent many long evenings telling Aeolus and his family about the war in Troy and of our adventures on the voyage. Before taking leave of Aeolus tonight, I spoke of my wish to return home safely, and asked for some favor to make this possible. Tomorrow we ship off.

Departure from Aeolus

This morning King Aeolus gave me as guest-present the hide of a nine-year-old ox containing all the ill winds. He secured it with a silver cord that would allow not a whisper of wind to escape. I fastened it to the hull of my ship, and we departed with the holds of our ships stocked with provisions.

Seventh month, second week: The green hills of Ithaca

We have sailed on friendly seas for nine days and nights. Today I sighted Ithaca and could even make out human forms and clearly see smoke. My mind at ease, I shall now sleep, for I have manned the sheets myself during the entire voyage, without anyone spelling me.

Seventh month, twenty-second day: Mutiny

I almost believe now that the hills of Ithaca appeared in a dream. They did not. It rends my heart to think I would be home this moment but for that short sleep of a week ago.

Eurylochus, my second in command, and the rest of my company are in profound sleep and darkness as I write of the events that return us to the shores of Aeolus.

*   *   *

Tonight, as we walked groggily from our ships, Eurylochus took me aside and advised me.

"Let the men rest tonight. They need sleep more than food, for their energies have been ravaged by storms. But you and I must build a fire and sit up awhile. I have things to tell you."

We sat by the campfire and I listened as Eurylochus began.

"While you slept, believing that in a few hours you would be in your homeland, I overheard the mates whispering:

'Why is it that wherever Odysseus goes, his hosts lavish him with priceless guest-gifts, while we leave

empty-handed? We shall have nothing but the scars of this endless voyage to bring our families when we return to Ithaca. Now, while he sleeps, let us seize that huge hide-skin filled with rare treasure from King Aeolus.'

"So saying, they loosed the cable that held the skin of ill winds. I was too weak against their mounting greed to stop them. Before I could shake you from your sleep, they had untied the silver cord and let loose angry winds and screaming squalls."

Eurylochus concluded and begged to be excused. He was senseless with exhaustion.

* * *

I remember how strongly I wanted to pitch myself overboard when I awakened to that tempest. Instead I drew the coverlet over my head and wept silently as I heard the men's oaths and the harsh blasts of the storm.

For many days and nights we were helpless victims of the most terrifying storms.

This blighted voyage, following hard on ten bitter years of war, is cause enough to warp the minds and jade the characters of my men.

End of seventh month: Banished from Aeolus

O Zeus, Marshall of the Waves, and Poseidon, Girder of the Earth, you have marked me and my men. Once again we are toiling the seas. There is no wind, so the crew must sap their strength at the oars. Early this morning, after a hearty meal, I and several of my mates set off for the palace to ask Aeolus to help us once more. The remaining men saw to the water butts and rigging.

I explained to the court in the most beseeching voice what had happened since we left three weeks ago. The king flared back with unexpected anger, calling us vile, doomed, and god-hated men. I left abruptly without opening my mouth—stricken dumb by his words.

Eighth month: Lamos

On the seventh day we arrived here in Lamos. I have secured my ship to this rock just beyond the bay, and wonder why my other captains have moored theirs so close together, far inside. There is no danger in this, however, since the waters here are calm and safe.

Worst disaster

I've lost everything—my ships, all my men. Only my black-prowed vessel and crew remain. We are down-hearted but take satisfaction in having been spared our lives, and for this we give hearty thanks. I record the sad events.

* * *

After we had moored our ships in the bay, I sent some men to scout Lamos. Not long afterward, two of the men came flying down the steep hill at terrific speed—running wildly toward the ship. Their shouting alerted us to look about for the cause of their alarm. Suddenly we spotted men of gigantic build on the precipice overhanging the bay. The next moment we heard the splintering of masts and the imploring cries of our fellows. The Laestrygones had hurled huge boulders on our fleet from the mountain-top, and all 11 ships with their crews sank together, leaving no trace.

I immediately cut loose the mooring on my ship. The men fell to rowing, the ship came about sharply, the sail

was hoisted, and we swiftly slipped into the open sea. No command had to be given. The men were grimly silent throughout.

One year completed

Some god has taken pity on us, at last. It is one year now that Zeus and Poseidon have vied with each other to become chief thunderer and destroyer of the Greeks.

I beached the ship and thought I would lay in rations first and explore the countryside later. But the men, not budging from their benches, silently sat and drew their cloaks over their heads. They were sick with grief, fatigue, and despair. Without disturbing them, I took my copper spear and went to explore the island.

From the top of a hill I could see in the distance a column of smoke. Assured that people lived on the island, I started back to the beach.

I hadn't gone far when I was startled by a sudden noise—a magnificent stag burst across my path. Every fiber in me tensed as I hurled my spear through his spine. It hit the mark. I recovered the deadly weapon and bound the four hooves with willow branches that I secured together in knots. I hauled the stag, steadying my progress with the spear. He was too large to carry across my shoulders in the customary fashion.

I stopped to rest a short distance from my ship and cheered my men by saying:

"We cannot be near Tartarus as long as this noble beast is ours."

Dropping their cloaks, they turned toward me.

Instantly they leaped into the surf and, as they admired the stag, washed their hands before preparing it for the fire.

At sunset we feasted on the succulent venison, washed down with long draughts of wine. My heart filled with hope as I looked upon my men's contented faces. I thanked the god who sent the stag across my path.

We are spending this calm night on the beach. Tomorrow at dawn I must hold council with my men. O Wise Athene, fortify and guide me. Forgive the Greeks for dishonoring your Temple. We were mad with victory last year and were not responsible for our actions.

First day of second year

I addressed my men this morning.

"Friends, I am without charts to navigate these unknown waters. I have no notion whether to sail east or west, nor do I understand the positions of the stars. If any of you can help me, speak now."

No one spoke. I then explained I had scouted the island and discovered signs of life. My men protested any further moves to seek out the natives, reminding me of the Laestrygones and the Cyclops. I spoke firmly, for I saw that to lose courage now would mean our end.

"Noble Greeks, you will not find yourself in the House of Hades before your time. Fear will never let you reach your homes in Ithaca. Eurylochus, take 22 men and I shall take the remaining 22. Then let one of us toss a coin and choose a copper side."

This was done, and it fell to tall Eurylochus to lead his men through the woods on their search. I remained behind with the rest.

Second year, second day: Aeaea

In this golden dawn, I am fully dressed to go to the goddess Circe's house. I have girted my copper sword and my long bow.

Eurylochus returned at sundown yesterday—alone! This godlike soldier was trembling with fear and begged me to quit the vile, enchanted land. He was out of his wits. It was long before any of us could learn what brought him to this state.

Eurylochus told us every detail of what had happened, but I shall hold my thoughts for the present, at least until I have seen for myself. No one would come with me today. Indeed, they tried to hold me back. But I must go after my men if I am ever to have peace.

I cannot take credit for overcoming Circe's magic. As I walked through the woods this morning, I met the god Hermes. He halted me, saying:

"Have you not learned your lesson, sharp-witted Odysseus? I can see by your sword and bow you are bound for Circe's and trouble. No mortal can withstand her magic. She will have you in the swinesty with your men. For you will find your men not men, but swine instead. They are strange beasts, having the form of swine and the mentality of men."

Only then did I believe what Eurylochus had told me, for the gods know all things. Hermes, noticing me lost in my private thoughts, spoke once more.

"Here is a solution! There is an herb that only the gods can pick. I shall give it to you and it will make you immune to her powerful magic potion."

He cast his eyes about and plucked from the ground a moly plant having black roots and a milk-white flower.

I took the moly and continued through the woods until I came to Circe's house. Bear, deer, and lions wandered about within the gates. They rushed eagerly to greet me in a manner unlike beasts, but peculiarly like men. There was a soft, sorrowful expression in their eyes that haunted me.

I stood outside the gates and called Circe's name. The lovely enchantress walked gracefully across the lawn to admit me herself. I followed her into the house, where she led me to a silver-cushioned throne. Sweet music filled the richly furnished halls. Circe offered me a golden

goblet of wine into which I dropped the moly. I drained its contents and as she waved her golden wand, I drew my sword.

"Circe, your magic is powerless. I have come for my men."

She dropped to her knees, believing I was a god. When her magic failed to change me into a swine, she was quick to obey my order and release my men.

Circe has honored me with favors and treated my men with kindness. I have beached the ship, and after much persuasion, asked the men and Eurylochus to join the rest of us.

Two years, one week: Departure from Aeaea

We have stayed one year at Circe's. My men have healed their storm-wrecked bodies and are restless to return home. I, too, am anxious to leave, but for more urgent reasons.

Circe loves me and would have me stay with her. This

fair-tressed goddess has restored hope and life in me, and my debt to her is deeply felt. But the anchors of my love and responsibility are not here; they are in Ithaca.

During this past year I have observed my men closely. Some behave with the rashness and abandon of sailors on foreign shores, but most do honor to their noble Greek names. Eurylochus has grown bitter and short-tempered. I feel a falling-away of our close friendship. I have frequently come upon him in thick talk with two or three men. My presence silences their whisperings.

Second year, eighth day: At sea

Dead—Elpenor, 26. My youngest soldier. A wild youth who accidentally fell from Circe's roof last night. Broken neck. Soul instantly left his body. Found this morning.

*   *   *

We put to sea as soon as Dawn spread her golden garment over the skies. The goddess made certain that our hulls were well stocked with provisions, including a large ewe and a prize ram. Circe stood on the shore, her hair bound in a veil, and wearing a gleaming silver dress. I watched her from the deck until she became a vapor on the sea mists.

I then turned to my men and told them that we were not bound for home but for Erebus on the rim of the earth. Here, in the Kingdom of the Dead, I must seek the prophet Tiresias, who will tell me all the events that have taken place in Ithaca and predict my safe arrival there. Circe has given me instructions for the voyage and the protection of the gods.

Second year, eighteenth day: The House of Hades

We reached Erebus by the water route. From the river Ocean, we entered the dark gates shaded by Persephone's poplars and willows. The land was bleak and dank. No light has ever smiled in this region.

I chose a patch of earth and dug a cubic square, and first poured in honey and milk, wine, and water. Then taking the ewe and ram, I beheaded them and let the blood pour into the hole, giving the carcasses to my men to burn on Ocean's shores. I offered prayers and promises of sacrifices to the dead souls.

My heart was full of dread in this land where no living man enters or returns. Wraithlike forms approached, a whole array—young, old, maidens, warriors. I was confused and repelled by their myriad faces.

The first who reached toward me was Elpenor, so recently dead. He begged me for a burial befitting a soldier. I promised on my return to favor his wish. So many crowded about to drink the sheep's blood—a special treat for dead souls—that I brandished my sword to ward them off. I waited until Tiresias made his way. I sheathed my silver-hilted sword. After he drank, he told me in these words:

"Odysseus, you come to these cheerless climes for advice on your safe arrival in Ithaca. I tell you that only after great hardship will you return home. Heed what I say: Poseidon will continue to stalk the seas after you, because you blinded his son, the Cyclops.

"But all is not hopeless. By overcoming human weakness, you have a chance of reaching your home. You will be forced to put in at the island of the sun-god Helios, who sees and hears everything. Beware that you leave his prize sheep and oxen unharmed! If you fail in this, I can promise you great hardship. Your ship and crew will be destroyed. You will survive, but will return home in a foreign ship to a palace greatly abused by Penelope's suitors. You will slay them, however—all 100 of them."

I have noted the prophesies of Tiresias. When he had finished, he disappeared into the shadows. I searched the crowd and recognized my mother. She came to drink the black blood. Looking up, she knew me instantly. She told me she had died while I was in Troy, and she, too, spoke of the suitors who live in the palace, eating up the food and lording it over my son, Telemachus. He idolizes me as one of the honored dead. My father, Laertes, has grown into the odd ways of the aged and lonely. He will soon die of longing for me, as did my mother.

When I reached out to embrace her, she drew back, telling me to go. Her body had been burned to ashes on the great funeral pyre. Only her soul escaped unharmed, and flew like a dove to this populous kingdom of Hades and awesome Persephone.

I saw many of the Greek heroes of the Trojan War, among them Agamemnon, who had escaped unharmed in the war. He spoke. His words were sharp and bitter. No wonder! He was slain by his wife when he returned home from the war. Nearby sat Minos, the ruling judge of the Underworld, his golden scepter in his hand. Giantlike Orion stalked the dark regions, just as he had on earth. But how can I write of the thousands that passed me? Many spoke and urged me to go back to the sun-blessed earth and remember them to the living.

Second year, second month: Back to Aeaea

We are once more on Aeaea. It was my solemn duty to perform funeral rites for the body of Elpenor, who begged me to grant this wish when I saw him in the Underworld. In our haste to leave this island 12 days ago, we had not time for this.

My men brought his body to the beach and we made a huge pyre on the hill. His armor, his oar, and other treasures were placed on the heap along with his body.

After the rites, Circe and her maidens brought large silver trays with food and wine for us. While my men slept, Circe told me of my voyage tomorrow. There are many dangers ahead for us. With Circe's good advice, we can avoid certain death—most of us, at least.

The Skurries

The Skurries are rocks on one side of a strait. The sea swells and empties against the Skurries with such force that lightning flashes garishly on the rocks. On the other side of the strait, two cliffs rise unevenly. Atop one of the peaks is an umbrella of snow that never melts and sheds darkness below. The cliff is as smooth as our fine pine oars. Halfway up is the cave of Scylla, a monster having six heads, who hangs over the side of her cliff to snatch fish, birds, or any living thing from the sea. From the side of the shorter cliff grows a wild fig tree. The terrible whirlpool, Charybdis, eddies at the ridge of the cliff, directly below the tree. No one, not even Poseidon, can escape the suction of her jaws. I have not told my men of the dangers that await us.

I begged them to remember their past courage. Once through the Skurries, we shall arrive at the Isle of the Sun. If we have survived the Cyclops, there can be no greater horror. These trials bolster our stamina. We are fortified by them, not weakened. And if it is our lot to fall, let it be said that the mighty have fallen, not the weak. Circe and Tiresias assured me we would reach home safely if we do as they say. We cannot falter now —the goal is too nearly within our grasp.

In spite of Circe's objections I am armed in full regalia, ready to attack the cannibal Scylla. Circe accused me of being a fool in attempting what the gods judge impossible for humans.

Threnacia, Helios' island

We are moored off the coast of the island of the sun. I can hear the bleating of sheep and the lowing of oxen. The sun-god Helios has 50 sheep and as many oxen that graze on this island's nap of green. Hearing the herds, I was reminded of Tiresias and Circe's warnings.

The courage of my soldiers has been driven to the snapping point. At this moment all their hearts combined cannot crack as mine. I see them all as one suffering face. I cannot bear to look at them. They have been silent for three days.

I repeated, "If we steal any of the god-prized herd, we will pay dearly."

At these words some wept, some swore oaths, others drew their cloaks over their heads. If they ignore my warnings we shall all perish. Since our luck has been so dogged, I urged that we turn about and leave this island. I begged them to consider this and make one mind on the matter.

While they are still considering this, I shall set down here what recent calamity has whitened their faces with terror, cast down their eyes, and silenced their tongues.

* * *

We first came to the region that the Sirens haunt. No man has ever returned from this island. No man has ever looked upon them. These sisters of song cast spells over men with their promises of full joy and rich wisdom. A man could not pass them without drawing closer to hear their honey-sweet song. But before he reached the Sirens, the song would rob him of life.

I devised a plan that would allow me to stay alive in spite of the Sirens' witchery. I had the men lash me to the mast and ordered them to sail past the island with all speed. I had my men's ears plugged with wax to make them dumb to the sorcery of the twin sisters. Mine were the only ears left unsealed. Stiffly upright, bound fast to the mast, I was tempted by such music that I struggled to be free. Eurylochus flew to the mast and several of the men helped him tighten my bonds.

I strained my eyes to see. There sat the Sirens atop mounds of skeletons, to whose dry bones still clung gray cobwebs of flesh. My desire to learn the wisdom of the worlds past and those yet to come was frozen by the grizzly sight. Neither joy nor wisdom did it bring, but the cold smell of death. Although I momentarily lost my senses, we passed through this danger without a hitch.

We breasted the waves smoothly. Suddenly we were drenched in dense clouds of mist and were almost at once in full view of the mountainous breakers crashing on the shore. Instinctively my men took to the oars. I paced the boards, grinding orders at them to keep their wits. They knew nothing of Scylla or Charybdis, nothing of the seething waters of the Skurries. I piloted them through the narrow pass in commands whose words are stamped everlastingly on my tongue.

"Hold fast to your oars, and you, at the sweep, allow a wide berth. Edge toward the cliffs under the overhanging crag. Look for the fig tree above the whirlpool and clear the breadth of its spread."

My men now had a clear view of the chasm caused by the breakers of Charybdis, and of the snake stream under

Scylla's cave. Oars were dropped and lost in the wake.

"Beat your oars and count together. We have less to fear here than we did in Cyclops' cave. Drop those oars and we'll fall off our course, capsize, and sink like a stone. Tomorrow we shall look back on this and marvel at our fear and rejoice in our courage."

I took my sword, and as we approached Scylla's cave I readied myself to lop off her heads. Traveling on winged oars, we skirted Charybdis and easily cleared the Skurries. I turned to look at my men. In that moment, Scylla swept down her hideous heads on coiled necks and snatched six of my bravest men from their benches.

*   *   *

This monstrous tragedy has put a pall on us. Worse still, there is a breach between us I cannot fathom. If they can ever agree to pass up this pastoral island of the sun, perhaps we may avoid the end-all disaster.

My men are still debating our plans. I can only hope they will remember my wisdom and courage.

Near the island of the sun

Eurylochus spoke for the men.

"Odysseus, you are tireless and have endurance unlike that of any other man. Certainly not any of us! We cannot spend another night on the black, boiling sea, and the winds bear signs of another storm.

"Our minds are made up. We say, stay the night here. Tomorrow let us leave at dawn. Now we need to eat, and we need sleep without the roll of the sea under us."

I was defeated. For it is our rule that the wish of the few must yield to the greater number. So be it.

We had provisions to last us several weeks. Before I made a move, I had them swear not to go near the sacred herds of the sun-god. Then we made for the island and beached the ship near a freshwater spring. The men ate well but soon fell to talking of their late comrades. Sleep, the great comforter, soon drove the dread thoughts of Scylla and Charybdis from their minds. We are to leave tomorrow. Dawn cannot come too soon.

The following day

We have just hauled our vessel into the cave, safe from the howling winds and squalls that mantle the sea and earth. We are secure. Early this morning, during the third watch, god-driven storms swept up from the south.

After hauling the ship in here, I called my men to a council. As soon as the sea calms and the skies clear, we will leave. How much longer can this storm plague me? I felt compelled to remind them once again of their oath. They humbly repeated it, and I was satisfied in their honesty.

Storms: Helios' island

For one month our private thoughts have dwelt on nothing but the tyranny of the South Winds. Now a greater tyranny is fast taking hold. Circe's provisions have dwindled to a mere bundle of scraps. There is still wine and corn. As long as these last, the cattle and sheep will be safe. Yet I fear that the temptation of the prize herds will be stronger than the promises of my men. Hunger blinds human reason.

I am sitting atop this hill, setting down my notes. Blessed peace and time to think. My men are off combing the shore and the beach for food. For Greeks who love the flesh of sheep and oxen, it is hard to take a diet of birds. We have even eaten fish. From this hilltop I can see for great distances around me. The sea is black, its surface ragged and tall as a mountain. I have just prayed, hoping the gods will show us a way out of our peril.

Treason

Our doom is sealed. Yesterday I fell asleep on the hilltop after my prayers. I awoke with renewed hope. Yet even while I slept, evil worked. In my absence, hunger drove Eurylochus to treason. He convinced the craven men that nothing was more hateful or dreadful than death by starvation. He led them first to offer prayers and sacrifices to the gods. They even vowed to build a temple to Helios when they returned to Ithaca. Then, breaking their oath to me, they captured the prized oxen.

They are now eating while more fresh meat, rolled on

a spit made of a thigh bone, is roasting over the fire. There is no wine left, but there is ample water from the fresh spring.

I'll not join in this feast of the dead. The torture of gnawing hunger is better than the vengeance of the gods. In this matter, Eurylochus and I disagree. He chooses death in one gulp. Well, he shall have it. Helios will never forgive my men, in spite of their prayers and sacrifices. May the gods have mercy on those who are doomed.

At sea

A black cloud as large as the Cyclopes' island hangs over our ship, and beyond are envious blue skies. The air and sea about us are as dim as Tartarus. My men hang on their oars. My lungs are filled with the damp, sharp scent of a hurricane. I smell death in the air. I dare not speak to my men. This morning, as soon as the seas calmed, we took the ship to sea. Six whole days my men had feasted on the oxen of the god.

Ogygia

It is two weeks since I last recorded the events of my homeward voyage. Although I no longer continue to hope,

I go on writing. I shall never return to Ithaca and my family.

I have been here five days. When I arrived, I was alone and but a shadow of my former self. Calypso, the nymph goddess, found me on the shore and brought me to her hollow cave. I bathed, was dressed in rich robes, and ate. Here all things are done in a manner befitting the immortal gods. This strange creature lives alone with her maids on this remote, god-forgotten island. It is populated by trees that lend beauty and rich fragrance to the island, and by birds that feed on the sea.

The gods never visit Ogygia. It is too isolated. In this remote place there are no cities where men may sacrifice oxen and sheep to the gods. There are no ships or men here to help me on my journey to Ithaca.

I spend my nights in the cave. My days here are used up on this shore. I am lost in grief and sorrowful memories.

* * *

Two weeks ago my entire crew was washed into the sea. My stout-ribbed ship was dismantled by violent winds and her pieces cast pell-mell on the waters. The death-tolling West Wind descended upon the ship shortly after we left the island of Helios. Under its first assault the stays snapped, toppling the mast and rigging. A falling block struck one of the men, instantly driving the life from his bones. Zeus then smote the ship with one of his white thunderbolts. The desperate men pitched into the deep and sank. The sundry parts of the ship vanished.

I grabbed a section of the mast wound round with rope, and straddled it. In this manner I rode the seas completely at the mercy of the winds. When the West Wind lost its force, the South Wind sent a fresh squall.

The next morning, to my dismay, I found myself the guest of Charybdis. She swallowed me and then spiraled me up to the tall fig tree, where I clutched a branch. There I hung fearfully until night, when she disgorged the mast. I dropped into the waves, regained my relic-craft, and paddled mightily with my hands in order to escape Scylla's gaping, greedy mouths.

I thank the gods that spared me. I grieve for the Greeks who have paid the high cost of this voyage.

This catastrophe, Calypso tells me, was the doing of the gods. Helios, when he discovered we had slaughtered and eaten his sacred herd, flew to Zeus in a rage, threatening to leave the earth and take the sun to the murky regions of the Underworld. To satisfy Helios, Zeus promised a white thunderbolt for the ship and

death for her crew. I alone was spared. I alone refused to eat the meat of the oxen and sheep.

Ninth year, end third quarter: Ogygia

The gods have not forgotten me.

For seven long years on this island I have brooded with no means of escape. I have been the captive guest of the strong-willed goddess Calypso. Today Hermes appeared before her with a command from Zeus to send me home. Bitterly she agreed to provide means for my voyage home. Yet she tried, even in the face of Zeus' command, to persuade me to stay. At supper tonight she said:

"Could you see into the future, you would find that the cup of your misfortune is not fully drained."

I cannot deny that I owe the fair goddess my life, for she found me a helpless, shipwrecked stranger on her shore. She has given me immortality and eternal youth, the gift of the gods. In spite of this, my desire to be home is the most precious gift of all. As for the dangers that await me, there is no mood, no pain, nor any torment I have not already faced on this voyage. I thank Zeus and the power that moved him. I know within that I am firm, for Calypso dares not disobey his order. Tomorrow I begin making a raft.

The raft is completed

There is nothing so invigorating to man's hope as hard labor. For four days I have felled trees, trimmed bark, split trunks, and fashioned a seaworthy craft that will

carry me on my voyage. Calypso gave me a copper-bladed ax and augers to drill holes for the lashings. We went to the end of the island to choose pines that have long since been sapless. I selected 20 trees so dry that they will buoy me high on the swell of the purple sea. It is a single-masted craft, complete with yard and sweep, and broad as a merchant vessel. Her stout sails I made with cloth from Calypso's loom.

The gods willing, I leave tomorrow at dawn.

Seventeenth day of voyage

Until this moment I could not leave off steering. For 17 days I have navigated with a close attention that has allowed me no relief or rest. At night I follow the course of the Great Bear and that mighty Orion, who never quite sinks beneath the ocean. Calypso has directed me to hold a course to the right of these constellations.

I have stopped to bring my record up to date. My voyage was blessed with fair and friendly winds. Just now I had my first view of land, a sight that brings with it a joy I have not felt in many years.

Ninth year, last quarter: Phaeacian palace

I am close to my journey's end. King Alcinous, my host and kinsman of Poseidon, has shown me every kindness and generosity a stranger could hope to expect. He has even promised me a ship and crew to take me safely to the shores of Ithaca. The Phaeacians are famous seamen and noted builders of worthy ships.

All of this generous hospitality comes after the last outrage of my tireless adversary, Poseidon. He very nearly brought to an ignoble end this weary and much-tried life of mine.

Events of the last five days

I had just gloried in the sight of land, rising like a shield from the sea mists, when winds from every direction wrenched me desperately across the waves. My courage was beginning to weaken when Ino, Goddess of the Waves, appeared before me, reproaching Poseidon for this unreasonable blast. She warned me to abandon the raft and gave me a scarf, saying that I could never sink so long as I wore it about my body. Then she departed beneath the waves.

Still I clung to the raft, for I suspected some plot to kill me. The tempest winds tore at my craft, and I plunged into the deep. My garments were dragging me down, making swimming difficult. After much effort, I rose to the surface, snatched a single timber from my raft, and while I sat astride it, tore the wet robes from my body. They were borne away on the waves—the royal robes given me by Calypso. I then bound Ino's scarf about my body and leaped into the black waters. My raft scattered across the swollen sea like dry leaves in an autumn wind.

At sunrise on the third day, I saw land. The wine-red sea suddenly calmed, yet I had barely the strength to swim. As I wearily approached the shore, I noted its rugged reefs and feared that one last wave would destroy my pain-racked body against their sharp teeth. My plans to evade them were interrupted by a mountainous wave that tore me from the waters headlong toward the hard jagged reefs. I snatched and clung to a spear of rock and escaped the crushing doom on the reefs. I held fast to the rock, moaning loudly, until the backwash of the wave carried me out a distance from the shore. I broke from the strong current and swam away from the reefs until I came upon the outlet of a fresh running river.

Thankful that this last peril of Poseidon's was won, I begged the gods to have mercy on me. I reached the shore all swollen and drenched with the scum and brine of the sea. I unwrapped the scarf to find this diary safely in its folds, where I had secured it. The scarf floated on the waters back to Ino, and I collapsed near the bank. When I awoke, the rays of the sun stretched down from the west. I despaired of what new harm awaited me in this unfamiliar country. The sea air was cold and damp, and

I knew that before night fell I would have to find shelter. I remembered Calypso's warning. I could endure adversity no more. This invocation to the gods fell from my trembling lips.

"Ye gods, all powerful and just, hear now my prayer. If my cup of misfortune is not yet empty, as Calypso said, and you choose to cut down this mighty oak, Odysseus, let justice be your guide and think how I have travailed to bring glory to the Greeks. The valor of Odysseus has rung out across the lands from the black towers of Troy. O that I had fallen with the flower of Greek manhood in Troy. Be just, O mighty gods! Spare me an ignoble death in this unfamiliar land."

Not far from the beach, I found a thicket with trees and mounds of dry leaves. I buried my body in one of the mounds, making a coverlet of leaves as warm as a sheepskin. And the gods sealed my eyes in sweet sleep.

The next day I was awakened by the sound of girls' shrill voices. It was my good fortune that the fair princess of this house was one of the girls. They had come

down to the river to do the laundry. In this land, noble ladies are trained to be useful. It was Nausicaa's duty to attend to the linen of the palace. Accordingly, the laundry, a basket of choice food and drink, a large purple ball for games, and a vial of olive oil to use if the girls should go bathing were loaded into a mule-driven wagon. Shielding myself behind the bushes, I could see the laundry spread out on the dry sand and the maidens racing after the ball that had been thrown near the surf. I broke off a leafy branch to cover myself and went to speak with them.

Princess Nausicaa was not alarmed by my wild, savage appearance. She ordered the frightened maids to fetch the olive oil and a tunic. They left these by the riverbank, where I could wash the salty crust of the sea from my body. When I returned to the lovely maidens, they gave

me drink and food, which I ate hungrily. Meanwhile, they packed the wagon with the neatly folded linen, hitched the mules, and were ready for the journey.

I followed a distance behind the chatterboxes and arrived at the palace shortly after. Nausicaa was most clever and charming. She explained that it would stir gossip among the good people if she returned to the palace in the company of such a striking-looking stranger.

* * *

I must stop now. It is late. Tomorrow I rise early.

Night of second day: Phaeacian palace

This king, this Alcinous, is made for all mankind and for all time. So deep is his wisdom, so sound is his affection, so large is his understanding, that all men may fully trust and love him. He has dedicated this day to my welfare and good, even though he does not know my name or that of my country. Tomorrow I sail for the land of my fathers with the bounty of his goodness as ballast for my stout galley.

This day has slightly dimmed the torture of the last 10 years—nay, 20 years. I am almost that same Odysseus who left 20 years ago for Troy. How often goodness reduces evil. Great wonder there is not more goodness in the hearts of men.

Just after dawn the king and I went to the meeting place in the city. A large company, including the other 12 Phaeacian kings, sat in council together on polished stone benches. Alcinous asked them to select a new ship and 52 oarsmen of great merit to take me to Ithaca. After

this, the kings and a large company gathered in the banquet halls of the palace for festivities. My ship was made ready, and her crew joined the company at the palace. Such a king is Alcinous, that he set a crown of hospitality on a stranger's head.

Kings, stalwart youths, and fair maidens thronged the banquet hall. Servants ran back and forth on the polished bronze floors bearing silver trays of steaming food, gold baskets of bread, and golden cisterns filled with wine. Twelve sheep, eight boars, and a pair of oxen were roasted over the fires.

Demodocus, a blind minstrel, was led to a silver throne beside the king. This divine minstrel brought song and poetry, the final perfection of a meal. When we had satisfied our appetites, Demodocus struck his lyre and sang a ballad that told of the feuding argument between

Achilles and Odysseus. What a bitter root, that helped to grow the bloody war of Troy! I was overcome with grief and drew my robe over my face. Alcinous saw my distress and, to draw me away from gloomy thought, ordered the assembled company to watch the games. We followed him through the halls to the outside arena.

The games began with a footrace, then wrestling, jumping, weight throwing, and finally, boxing. The sturdy Laodamas, son of Alcinous, won the boxing match. He approached me soon after, saying, "I have noticed your hands and mighty physique. They mark a man of power who has performed feats of strength. You have been through grave times, yet you are in your prime. Pray, let us see a sample of your strength."

I begged to be excused. My spirit and body were not fit for competition with these stalwarts. My mind was still morose. I was in no humor to accept this challenge. I declined the honest Laodamas. Another youth chided me and accused me of being a merchant who peddled his wares on the sea for the sake of gaining a large profit. I sprang up glaring at the mere chip. What he possessed in physique he lacked in mind. I seized a weight larger than any that had been hurled, and flung it. It sang through the air, landing farther than the others. One clear voice rose above the thousands in the arena, saying that no one could equal my mark, much less exceed it.

I turned to the athletes and invited any of them to challenge me — all except Laodamas. That would have offended him. In truth I felt assured of victory, for the Phaeacians are no match for a Greek. They are excellent runners and skilled seamen, lovers of good food and clothes, and especially are they talented dancers and musicians. So Alcinous, wishing to leave me with high praise for their endeavors, summoned the dancers to demonstrate their skill. Demodocus accompanied the youths on his silver lyre. Fleet of foot, light of movement, they were outstanding. In one of the dances, two of Alcinous' sons, using a purple ball, mixed sport and dance in the most graceful and intricate steps I have seen. I watched amazed. Truly they are marvelous.

Noting my satisfaction, Alcinous called the brash youth who had insulted me. He apologized and presented me with a silver-wrought sword and an ivory scabbard to atone for his rudeness. Then Alcinous asked his wife to fill a beautiful chest with the finest tunics and mantles as guest-gift for me. He turned to the 12 kings, requesting

that they, too, prepare chests filled with finely loomed clothing, and besides, give talents of gold. The kings promptly left, to return later for feasting and the presentation of gifts. I cannot help but think how honored and respected I shall be when I return to Ithaca with these rich gifts.

The games were over. We returned to the palace to prepare for the final feast. A large copper cauldron was filled with hot water for me and I bathed. I dressed in a noble tunic and mantle presented to me by the gracious queen. Not since Calypso have I reveled in such luxuries of the gods.

I must leave now to join the good Phaeacians in feasting and the showing of gifts. This being my last day here Princess Nausicaa has just said her farewell to me. I shall never forget this maiden, so full of charm and wit. This gentle girl has given me life. When I return to Ithaca, I shall pay her the homage of a goddess.

Third night: Homeward bound

This stout ship courses the waves as lightly as a gull skirts the sea. I am reclining on deck. A brilliantly colored carpet and a sheet have been spread for my comfort. I am a king returning home in noble style — with a hardy crew and a trim ship stowed with rich treasure. But a mightier king — Poseidon, the Earth-shaker — is at the helm. For no craft has parted the rolling sea as smoothly and swiftly as this vessel.

* * *

Last night Alcinous continued his rites of hospitality until twilight. At dawn we stowed the copper cauldrons, the gold, and the coffers filled with rich raiment. Then we returned to the palace for sacrifices to Father Zeus, patron of all suppliants. By this time I had grown anxious to be off. During the ceremonies and speeches, I could not help watching the sun, urging it westward, as a farmer does while he tills the earth from sunup to sunset. He toils until the sun reaches the western horizon. Then his heart rejoices to go home for supper.

These festivities and the hoards of people are wearisome. Except that I never tire of listening to Demodocus, who sang a lay of the city of Troy last night. He sang as if he had actually seen the great timber horse Athene had designed for us. He told how I, Odysseus, brought the horse, its belly filled with Greek

soldiers, up to the gates and left it there. And how the Trojans dragged the instrument of their destruction within the mighty citadel. Once more I tried to hide my deep distress. Alcinous stopped the god-gifted bard and spoke encouragingly of tomorrow's voyage.

"Now tell us, noble stranger, whither you are bound, that we may know where to direct our prow. Our Phaeacian ships are unlike any other ships. They navigate without steersmen. They are never lost at sea, nor have they suffered the destruction of winds or storms. And, although Poseidon does not approve of our giving safe voyage to every stranger on these shores, we do willingly send you home with our escort and our gifts. Tell us your country, the name given you by your father, and how long you have been away. Have you lost a kinsman in the war, or perhaps a friend, that these minstrel songs move you to tears? What places have you visited before reaching our lovely shores?"

It was the moment for me to stand before my deeply kind host and express full thanks for his royal welcome. Demodocus sat with his back to a column, listening and watching without seeing. I bent my courtesy first in his direction. It is proper for a man of understanding and knowledge of the world to show a reverence and regard for poetry. I then spoke to the large company.

Once I had begun, I was in full control again of an eloquence of speech formerly my custom to use. I told them of Ithaca, and in the telling I remembered anew things I had thought forgotten. I stood there, a minstrel, spinning magic words of his own history. My own ears listened with freshness to the adventures and the long chain of woe — the Cyclops, the Laestrygones, Circe, the Underworld — every element, every detail of my incredible voyage. In this manner we spent the night until the rays of this day fell upon my hushed audience.

* * *

The circle is brought full round. I have ended my tale and my journey home at once. A heaviness of sleep disobeys my desire to hail the first sight of the familiar slopes of Mount Neriton on Ithaca.

O Zeus, mighty governor of men and gods, unseal my eyes again only to discover the familiar halls of my home and the beloved faces of my son and wife. Snip with mighty shears the threads of my despair. Acknowledge that I, Odysseus, Warrior King of Ithaca, have endured misfortune with dignity and unstinting love for the gods.

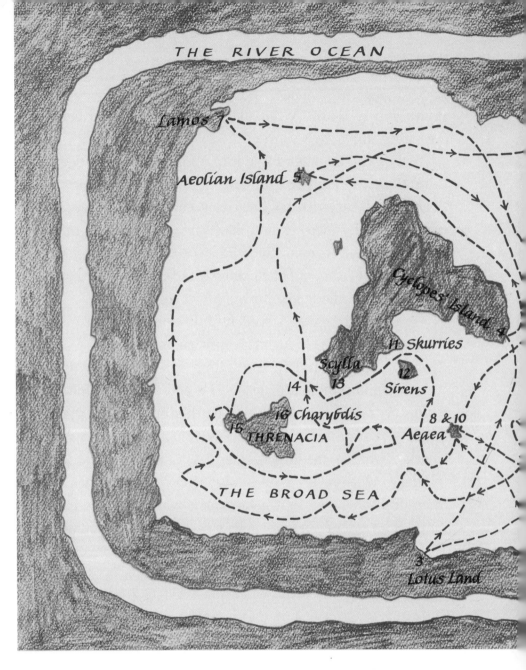

THE RIVER OCEAN

Lamos 7

Aeolian Island 5

Cyclopes' Island 4

11 Skurries

Scylla
13

12
Sirens

14

16 Charybdis

15
THRENACIA

8 & 10
Aeaea

THE BROAD SEA

3
Lotus Land

ODYSSEUS'
NAVIGATION
CHART

1 Ismarus – Land of the Cicones.
2 Cape Maleia – Strong currents
   and winds drive Odysseus' ships
   off course.
3 Lotus Land – Lotus Eaters.
4 Cyclopes' Island – Home of the
   one-eyed giants.
5 Aeolian Island – King Aeolus,
   guardian of the winds.

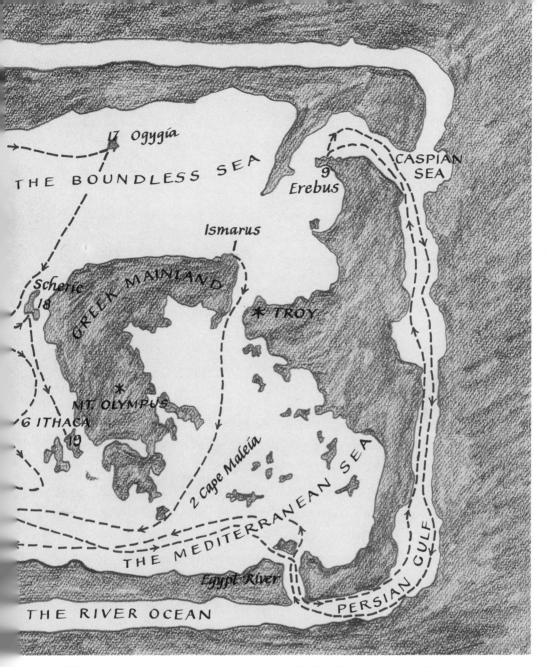

THE BOUNDLESS SEA

17 *Ogygia*

CASPIAN SEA

9 *Erebus*

Ismarus
1

Scherie
18

GREEK MAINLAND

★ TROY

MT. OLYMPUS

6 ITHACA

19

2 Cape Maleia

THE MEDITERRANEAN SEA

PERSIAN GULF

Egypt River

THE RIVER OCEAN

6 Ithaca – sighted from ship.
7 Lamos – Land of the Laestrygones.
8 Aeaea – Circe's Island.
9 Erebus – Realm of perpetual darkness and land of the dead.
10 Aeaea – Return visit to Circe's island.
11 Skurries – jagged, rocky reefs.
12 Island of the Sirens.

13 Scylla – six-headed monster.
14 Charybdis – huge whirlpool.
15 Threnacia – Isle of the sun god.
16 Charybdis – Odysseus returns alone.
17 Ogygia – Calypso's remote, desolate island.
18 Scherie – Land of the Phaeacians.
19 Ithaca – Odysseus returns to his homeland.

AS THE MASTER MARINERS reached Ithaca, the morning star rose. The ship's deep prow emerged from the sea onto solid earth. Still, godlike Odysseus slept soundly. The crew left their oars and, taking the corners of the soft carpet, lifted the king. They carried him to an olive tree situated near a cave, where they left him, surrounded by the copper cauldrons, the treasure of gold, and the chests of finely loomed clothing. Certain that their royal charge was sheltered from the cold winds and a safe distance from the plunderers of the road, the crew returned to the ship. The fifty-two men cast off, flashing their oar blades over the dark waters.

Vigilant Poseidon watched with vexation the flawless return of Odysseus to his kingdom. For Poseidon had promised long ago to punish the Phaeacians for allotting their prized ships to every suppliant who came to their

shores. He counseled with his brother Zeus and immediately decided to carry out his final act of judgment. Odysseus was god-protected by Zeus and Athene. The Phaeacians, then, would feel Poseidon's wrath, proving that mortals may not slight a god.

As the Phaeacian ship neared its homeland once again, the best of ships was turned into a rock measured in shape and size like itself. Poseidon then encircled the city in shadow-casting hills. The Phaeacians witnessed all this with wonder. But Alcinous bowed his head, obedient to the fulfillment of the ancient prophecy. Henceforth the Phaeacians would guard their seamen and ships more carefully.

A dozen bulls were sacrificed to Poseidon that he might relent from enshadowing the bright land of the Phaeacians. And as they gathered round the sacrificial fires, Odysseus on faraway Ithaca stirred from his deep sleep.

THE EAGLE
AND THE GEESE

THE BEGGAR and the swineherd climbed the steep path leading to the city and soon approached a clear fountain surrounded by black poplar trees. The citizens of Ithaca drew their water here, and every traveler stopped to refresh himself and to pay homage to the Nymphs' Altar fixed into a crag of the fountain.

Melanthius was driving his choice goats to the palace. He met the beggar and the swineherd at the fountain and made no secret of his loathing.

"What a droll pair! One pig leading another pig. How often have I seen such a sack of rags as this beggar, his back to a pillar and scratching while whining for scraps of food. I can tell you what to expect at the palace of Odysseus. Flying footstools will graze that hangdog head or crack those brittle ribs," sneered Melanthius, kicking the beggar for extra measure of his contempt.

The beggar, who was no ordinary beggar, as Melanthius would soon learn, turned to the Nymphs' Altar.

"O Fountain Nymphs, hear my plea. Let Odysseus return to Ithaca without delay and put an end to this fraud who plays henchman to the suitors."

"Hear this cur! This vermin carrier! Would you cast a curse on me?" demanded Melanthius with a sudden start. "O Apollo, strike the heart of Telemachus today. The suitors will then demand Penelope's hand and end their lingering song of love, once and for all time."

And so, having stopped at the fountain and paid homage to the gods, both parties took their separate paths to the palace of Odysseus. Melanthius, taking the shorter one, arrived ahead of the beggar and the swineherd.

The beggar paused to admire the magnificent building, its trellised courts, and its richly wrought gates. A dog, lying not far away and trembling all over with ticks, suddenly raised its weary head and wagged its tail. It had not the strength to move toward the beggar. The beggar saw the dog, and brushed away a tear.

The swineherd, who was none other than Eumaeus, the trusted servant of Odysseus, turned to the beggar. "That is Argos, the hound Odysseus left behind when he sailed for Troy. It has fallen ill now that its master has failed to return after these twenty years," he explained as he entered the palace.

After catching sight of the beggar, Argos sank to the ground and died. The beggar hastened into the palace and crouched at the entrance to the Great Hall. Telemachus saw him there and handed Eumaeus a loaf of bread and portions of meat. "Here, pass these to the beggar. Tell him that if he chooses to be timid, then he will surely starve," he said.

The beggar gratefully took the victuals from Eumaeus and put them in his wallet. From where he sat he could hear the bard's voice above the loud bantering of the suitors.

Each day the suitors came to the palace with rich gifts for Penelope, each hoping to gain favor in the queen's eye. But she rarely appeared before them. Putting them off in this way, the queen only made them more spiteful. The swarm of suitors installed themselves in the banqueting hall, eating and drinking, and lording it over the servants and Telemachus.

The goddess Athene made the beggar bold and encouraged him to beg scraps from the heaping tables. Imitating the pose of a professional mendicant, the upturned palm stretched forward, the beggar made his way among the suitors. Some were moved to pity; all were taken by surprise and wondered who the pitiful figure was. Melanthius explained.

"He is led to this noble company by none other than the pig man, Eumaeus. I ran into the riffraff at the Fountain of the Nymphs. Beware of this cucumber, for his tongue is not vegetable. If you had heard his prayer to the nymphs, noble Greeks, your hearts and knees would tremble."

Antinous turned to Eumaeus with these angry words: "How dare you bring every flea-laden beggar to prey on our generosity and lenient hearts. This limp rag, this killjoy, spreads gloom and hard luck wherever he goes. If each suitor would give you a taste of this generosity I give you now, we would be rid of you." And so saying, he balanced his footstool on his toe and took it up in his hand.

The beggar drew himself to his full height and his voice rang out defiantly. "It is a pity your manners are not a fair copy of your handsome face."

"Take this for your impudence!" shouted Antinous as he hurled the footstool.

The beggar was unmoved as a solid rock by the blow. He returned to the entrance and put his wallet, bursting with food and alms, on the threshold. With determined control he turned to the suitors and spoke.

"Hear me, Strangers! I am a man who was once rich with a houseful of servants. My gates were open to all — poor and rich alike. Zeus saw fit to strip me of my wealth and position when I was taken by pirates to the land of the Egyptians. An alarm warned the people. They rose against my captors and sent them scurrying for safety. I was left behind and sent to Cyprus as a slave. I come from Cyprus as you see me now, free only to roam and beg my way in a strange land."

He turned directly to Antinous and continued. "This animosity of yours, Antinous, does not become a man of breeding, for it is based on the most vile human weakness — satisfaction of the belly. If the gods are just, the hungry poor shall see Antinous dead before his wedding day."

"Stop, or you shall answer for your words by being dragged hand and foot until your limbs are turned to ribbons," threatened Antinous.

"Antinous, by your unnatural rudeness to this beggar you have sealed your doom. The gods themselves visit us disguised as beggars to test our human kindness here on earth," protested the other lords.

Word of the disgraceful behavior reached Penelope. The suitors were all hateful to her, but Antinous was the embodiment of evil in her eyes. She summoned Eumaeus to her room and made inquiries concerning the beggar.

"Kind Eumaeus, who is this beggar that has suffered such insults in the house of Odysseus? We have need of the master to save us all from ruin. He, with his son Telemachus, would make full payment for these outrages."

When she had finished, Telemachus sneezed, so that the palace echoed with the sound. "Hark how my son replies with that sneeze. It means that the gods have heard me, and what I have said will happen according to their will."

And returning to the subject of the beggar, the queen continued, "Now tell me of the beggar, that I may make amends in defense of my lord Odysseus."

"O Fair Queen, if you could hear his story, you would fall into a trance with its telling," began Eumaeus. "His deeds are worthy of the bard's god-given gifts. For three days and nights he sat by my fire and told me the tale of his misfortune. He is distantly related to Odysseus, of the race of Minos in Crete. I was the first to welcome him to Ithaca, for he came to me fresh from his ship."

Eumaeus promised to bring the beggar to her the next day. He hastened downstairs to Telemachus and whispered in his ear, "Master, I must leave to look after the swine that are both your interests and mine. Bear yourself like a man and take every caution with these evil plunderers of your house."

"Go, Eumaeus, but return early tomorrow with stout beasts as sacrifice to the immortal gods," Telemachus said softly.

The evening meal was followed by great merriment. Song and dance filled the night air. There suddenly appeared a true beggar, a young country bumpkin who sponged his living about Ithaca. This glutton, whose nourishment turned to flab and sloth, was called Irus.

This evening he was bribed by the suitors to taunt the beggar and turn him out of the palace. He stood thickly in the entrance and steadily eyed the beggar. "Move, and let your betters pass, or you will find yourself sprawled on the porch floor."

"I fail to see a better one than I. In fact, I find only you, a man like myself, made to wander from house to house for food," replied the beggar in an even voice. "Let us not fight," he added, leveling his eyes with the tramp's, "lest my blows to your face make a ruddy bib of blood on your chest."

"By Zeus!" snapped the young beggar. "Were it not for your beard, I would swear by your cackle that you were an old crone. Now which of my blows would best suit you? I think the double-fisted hammer blows will drop your teeth to the ground like seeds of corn. Put up your fists, ancient crone. I will teach you not to provoke a young man to fight you!"

The loud argument caught the attention of the

roistering suitors. They crowded around the boxers and
made a sport of the affair.

"Look, starving jacks, there on the spit roasts a prize
ox. I offer the best picking to the victor of this boxing
match and he will always be free to beg in this palace,"
coaxed Antinous.

"Noblemen, I am too old and wearied by hardship to be
fighting a young man. But the necessity of eating urges
me to stake a claim for the prize," said the beggar meekly.

An area was cleared in the Hall, and the rivals made
ready for the match. The beggar removed his rags and
bared his massive thighs, powerful chest and shoulders,
and brawny arms.

"To think these rags kept secret such a monument of
a body!" remarked the suitors in amazement.

When Irus saw that the old beggar was a man of girth
and steel, he turned white with fear. This would be a fight

he had not bargained for. Never again would he play the bully.

"Now, Irus, you ton of loose flesh, if you lose this fight, I shall exile you to King Echetus, the enemy of mankind," threatened Antinous sharply.

Meanwhile, the beggar was considering the best method to beat the quivering Irus. Would it be better to kill him outright with one resounding blow, or should he merely rap him and knock him out? He decided in favor of mercy. Irus struck the beggar on the shoulder and in turn was rapped on his jaw. The bone cracked and maroon blood gushed from his nose and mouth. Irus fell, biting the dust in agony and beating his feet into the ground in a fit.

A roar of laughter broke out as the beggar dragged the shrieking Irus out to the courtyard. He propped him up against the gate and thrust his walking staff into his hand. "There, frighten the hounds of Hades, scarecrow! Let that be a lesson to you never again to play the king of beggars."

When he returned to the Hall, Eurymachus baited him before the others. "We are honored to have such a shining light among us. Note how polished his head is, with not one thread of hair left. Stranger, for you have not a name, would you care to be my slave? Build dikes of dried bricks or plant trees in exchange for food, clothing, and leather? But you are an idler and would rather beg than do an honest man's work."

"And you are a braggart full of your own importance in the company you keep," the beggar shot back. "If Odysseus were to appear now, that door would be as a keyhole, so fast would all of you rush to escape his wrath and vengeance."

"Vain cock! Do you think your victory over this scapegoat, Irus, entitles you to strut and insult us before our own eyes?" thundered Eurymachus, flinging a footstool in the beggar's direction. The beggar ducked, and it struck the hand of a cupbearer who dropped to the ground in agony.

"O that this troublesome stranger had died before causing such discontent and pain. This is the beginning of his malice and the end of our pleasure," despaired the suitors.

Late that evening the suitors left the palace after plundering it of food and peace. Telemachus called to Eurycleia, Odysseus' old nurse. "Mother, see that the women remain in their rooms while I strip the walls in the Hall of my absent father's war gear. They have grown brown with soot and dirt, and I fear will rot away."

"But the women should hold the torches so that you may have light to do this work," protested the old woman.

"This beggar can earn his keep by helping me," replied Telemachus shortly.

Eurycleia left the men alone. The beggar sprang up to help the young master unhook the helmets, spears, and shields from the walls. Athene held high a golden lamp that lighted their secret task wondrously.

"See how the walls and pinewood framing glow. Surely this light is sparked by an immortal god," marveled Telemachus.

"It is not for you to question miracles, my son," warned the beggar moodily. "Get to bed and leave me here to think."

* * *

Penelope was restless this ominous night. She told one of her maids to cover a stool by the fire with a sheepskin and summon the beggar to her room.

When the beggar appeared before her, she said, "Stranger, tell me your name and your country."

"Madam, you may ask me any other question but those two questions," replied the stranger uneasily.

He did, at last, make up a tale of his life designed to please and satisfy her woman's curiosity. The lonely

queen was so grateful that Eurycleia was called to bathe his feet.

"Eurycleia, bathe this man. Perhaps somewhere someone is doing a similar kindness to your master, Odysseus."

The nurse turned to the stranger and said, "For the queen's sake I shall wash your feet, Stranger, but not for hers alone. I do this for your own sake, so like in build and voice are you to Odysseus."

She filled the footbath with water, not once taking her eyes from him. His heart stopped beating, as a sudden fear gripped him. The scar on his foot, made by a boar when he was a youth, was as familiar to the nurse as her own hand.

The old woman took his foot, her fingers gently feeling the scar. The foot slipped into the tub and splashed water all over the floor. The expression on her old face was a mixture of joy and sadness.

"You are my own Odysseus," she managed to whisper.

She turned toward Penelope to announce the great news, but Penelope's gaze was lost in the flames on the hearth. Odysseus pulled Eurycleia to him, his hand on her throat.

"Hush, no one knows or shall know who I am until such time as I see fit. Only Telemachus knows. I told him when he came to Eumaeus' lodge two days ago. Dear nurse, seal this secret in your woman's heart that has loved me from the moment of my birth."

On the opposite side of the hearth, Penelope stirred in her ancient chair of silver and ivory. "There is a matter I wish to discuss with you, honored sir. You have witnessed how the palace is overflowing with ravenous princes and lords. They have treated you with their customary bad manners. In truth, it is I who am responsible for their ill humor. For more than three years they have come each day to the palace expecting me to choose one of them for my husband. I promised that I would make up my mind when I had finished weaving a shroud for my husband's father, Laertes. Each day that I kept these unwelcome guests waiting, they became more contemptuous. Recently they have discovered my secret. I would weave the shroud during the day and unravel it at night. I vainly hoped this would discourage them and that they would leave my son and me in peace. They refuse to wait any longer, and now even my father and Telemachus insist that I come to a decision.

"But pray you listen to this dream I have had and see what meaning you discover. There are twenty wild geese on my estate that feed on the golden corn. In this dream, a large eagle swept down and killed all twenty of the geese. I sobbed for my dearly loved geese. Suddenly the eagle spoke. 'This is as it shall all happen one day, and no dream. I am Odysseus and the geese your suitors.' "

"Gentle Queen, this is a dream foretelling the destruction of the suitors — none excepted," said the beggar.

"Alas," she sighed, "who can tell the true purpose of dreams? I only know that tomorrow I must choose a husband. For this purpose I have planned an archer's contest. The man who will wed me must be able to string

Odysseus' great bow and send it through twelve axes. If such a man lives, then he will take Odysseus' place."

"O honored wife of Odysseus, do so arrange this great test. I can promise you that your master will himself be there to send that arrow through the eyes of the axes," the beggar assured her.

"I thank you, Stranger, for your expressions of hope and comfort," said the queen wearily. "And now to a sleep that will drain my cares away. I have wept myself to sleep since Odysseus left to destroy that infamous city whose name I never mention."

The next morning Penelope and her maids-in-waiting descended the long stairway leading to the depths of the palace. She unlocked the chamber where the famed bow of Odysseus hung. Unhooking the bow herself, she carried it and the quiver of arrows to the Great Hall. The maids-in-waiting carried the iron axes and flanked either side of the queen. She spoke in a steady voice.

"Here, noble Princes, is the bow of Odysseus. I now declare the contest open that will decide who among you will wed me."

Telemachus dug a trench and arranged the axes in a long line. He then pounded the earth with his foot, making the ground firm around the oak handles. When he had finished, he ordered the suitors to take their turns at the bow.

Meanwhile, Odysseus followed Eumaeus and the servant Philoetius into the courtyard. Showing the scar on his foot as positive proof, he told them he was Odysseus. Then the crafty king explained his plan.

"Let us return to the Hall separately. The suitors will never think to pass the bow to me, but you, Eumaeus, must make this gesture. Then go directly to the women's quarters and instruct them to remain there. Whatever noise or cry they hear from the Hall must not prompt them to leave. Philoetius, go you to the gates and fasten them securely — not one of the suitors must escape. Do this, and as reward I shall see both of you wed to honorable women and provide you with homes and chattel. You will be freedmen to live as equals with me for the rest of your days."

Odysseus returned to the contest and was soon followed by Eumaeus and Philoetius. Eurymachus was warming the bow over the fire. "It is no use! I cannot bend this bow to string it. I, along with the other suitors, am disgraced by this test of my strength and must forfeit the fairest lady in the realm," he despaired.

"Do not weaken so soon in this contest, Eurymachus," urged Antinous. "Tomorrow is the feast of the god-archer, Apollo. We shall have Melanthius bring his choice goats to the palace as sacrifice to Apollo. For the present, let us pass the wine and offer our cups in libation to the god."

"Hear me, Prince Eurymachus, and especially you, Prince Antinous," began Odysseus. "You show wisdom in favoring tomorrow for your trial of the bow. Therefore you will lose nothing, for the moment, by letting me try my skill with that curved bow."

"Old man, do not presume to challenge the younger generation," flared the outraged Antinous.

"Antinous, your manners are villainous in another man's home," said Penelope with indignation. "This man has no designs in his heart to carry me off as his wife. Vile man, do not vex me with your base thoughts."

"Mother, you speak out of turn," said Telemachus. "The bow is man's business, and as master of this house it is my place to step in and settle this argument. Go to your room and occupy yourself with woman's duties — weaving, spinning, and seeing to your maids." Then turning to the swineherd he commanded, "Eumaeus, give the beggar the bow."

Eumaeus carried the bow to Odysseus and put it in his hands. He then sought the nurse and taking her aside whispered, "Telemachus orders you to lock the doors of the women's quarters, and be sure no one leaves."

She fumbled and muttered in agitation as she hurried off, shutting and fastening the doors behind her. As she carried out these commands, Philoetius crept stealthily into the courtyard to fasten the gates. He returned as softly to his stool and sat watching.

Odysseus was testing the bow, turning it over and over, examining it closely for woodworms or damage. Everyone sat silently absorbed in his expert handling of the bow.

"See how he checks the instrument, or is the beggar making the bow?" mocked one of the suitors.

Satisfied that it was sound, Odysseus strung the bow and flexed it with his customary ease. Then he plucked the string, and it rang. All this was done with the ease of a musician who tightens a gut on his lyre and plucks it to prove its tone.

Zeus, at that moment, sent a peal of thunder from Mount Olympus. Odysseus thanked him for this good omen, but the suitors exchanged pale looks of amazement and felt a chilling uneasiness. The warrior king then snatched an arrow, brought the bow to full draw and let drive. The arrow flew flawlessly through the axes. Not one axe was undone.

"Telemachus, I have made myself worthy of your great generosity," exclaimed Odysseus, taking his place on the throne. "While it is still daylight, order the evening meal, for we shall have entertainment afterwards more fitting than dancing or singing." He threw a look of deep

meaning to his son, who fastened his sword and sprang
to his father's side.

Odysseus shed his rags and in one leap stood in front
of the entrance. He emptied the quiver of arrows on the
floor and boomed out, "Finally, finally the sham of this
disguise, invented by Wise Athene, is shed. By Apollo, I
see a target before me never struck till now!"

The target raised a golden cup of wine to his lips,
unaware that as he drained its contents, he, Antinous,
would as swiftly be drained of life.

"Stranger, your flesh shall be picked by hungry
vultures for the murder of this prince of Ithaca's

manhood," Eurymachus protested as the arrow struck Antinous in the neck.

"Vile wasters, you have ravaged my home of provisions, vainly wooed my wife, and heartlessly plotted to kill my son, Telemachus." Odysseus warned them, "I am here now to avenge these crimes."

Terror raced through their guilty hearts. Eurymachus alone found courage to speak. "If you are Odysseus, then guilty we are. The originator of these crimes lies there dead. Love for Penelope was the outward sign of Antinous' secret ambition to be king of Ithaca, and toward this end he even plotted to kill Telemachus. He was your only enemy, and we are still your weak subjects — ready to repay you and give loyal support to you."

"Eurymachus, all your wealth combined will not sway me one inch. You will all pay with your lives — not one drop of blood will be spared," thundered Odysseus, the fierceness of his glare withering all hope in the suitors' hearts.

The next to fall was Eurymachus. Odysseus then let his arrows fall as the rain of death. The suitors' shrill cries rose to the beams as they dropped lifeless to the ground. Only one in the company was spared. It was the bard who had been hired by the suitors to entertain them against his good will.

Odysseus spied someone wrapped in an oxskin and crouched under the throne. He drew his arrow. The object crawled toward Telemachus, and throwing aside the oxskin, embraced his knees.

"Telemachus, it is I, Medon, your guardian and

companion through your boyhood. Beg your father to spare me," pleaded the discreet Medon.

Telemachus nodded to his father. Odysseus smiled, saying, "For Telemachus' sake are you saved. Remember and preach this wherever you go: The gods defend the upright but destroy the weak. Now you and the bard wait in the courtyard, away from all this ugly carnage."

Eurycleia was summoned to the Hall and found Odysseus spattered with blood, like a lion who has slain and gorged himself on an ox. Eurycleia let out a battle cry when she saw that all the suitors were slain.

"Hold your cry, good woman. It is disrespectful to rejoice over death. Bring me brimstone, and light the fires."

When the fire had been purified by the brimstone, Eurycleia hastened to her mistress and told her the news. Penelope returned with the nurse, not knowing whether to flee to her husband and embrace him or to conduct herself with caution until she was certain that the stranger was indeed her husband.

Odysseus sat there, his eyes downcast, waiting for his wife to cry out to him. She drew back shyly.

"Mother, are you cruel or coldhearted? Is this the welcome my father deserves after all these years of hard waiting?" Telemachus demanded.

"My son, there is such an argument and stirring in my heart that no strength is left to speak or move."

"Leave us, Telemachus," said Odysseus smiling. "After I have cleaned and properly attired myself, your mother and I can sit by the fire and in our own way understand each other."

GLOSSARY

ACHILLES [uh KIL eez], the bravest and one of the most colorful Greek heroes in the Trojan War. He once had the choice of living a long but inglorious life or a short, heroic one. He chose the heroic life. Later, in the Underworld, Achilles told Odysseus he would rather be alive as a slave than be a king in the Underworld. When Achilles was killed in the Trojan War, his priceless armor went to Odysseus.

AEAEA [ee EE uh], the island in the Tyrrhenian Sea where Circe lived.

Odysseus and his men lived on Aeaea for one year.

AEOLUS [EE uh lus], son of Poseidon, and God of the Winds. It was Aeolus who gave Odysseus a hide-skin containing all the ill-winds so that he could reach Ithaca safely.

AGAMEMNON [ag uh MEM non], leader of the Greek forces in the Trojan War. Agamemnon was the only Greek leader to reach home safely and triumphantly. The other leaders were victims of the vengeful Olympian gods, who tormented the Greeks after the fall of Troy.

ANTINOUS [an TIN oh us], the boldest and most arrogant of Penelope's suitors.

ANTIPHAS [AN tuh fus], the son of an aged counselor in Ithaca and the brother of one of Penelope's suitors. Antiphas and five other men went to the cave of Polyphemus and were barbarously eaten.

APOLLO [uh POL oh], God of Light, Truth, Music, and Healing. Like his sister Artemis, he was a master archer. Next to his father, Zeus, Apollo was the most important of the Greek gods. He played an important role in the lives of men, and for this reason many temples were built in his honor. One day of every week—Sunday—was set aside for honoring the sun god.

ATHENE [uh THEE nee], Goddess of Wisdom and the Arts, War and Peace. She was also protectress of Athens, the most outstanding Greek city in the ancient world and the capital of modern Greece. It was in the Temple of Athene in Troy that a Greek soldier laid violent hands on a priestess. Athene invoked Zeus to avenge her.

AURORA [uh ROHR uh], the beautiful Goddess of Dawn. The Greeks believed she opened the gates of day every morning to let Apollo through with the sun.

CALYPSO [kuh LIP soh], the nymph goddess who lived on the remote island of Ogygia. Odysseus remained on this island for seven years, until Calypso helped him to resume his voyage home.

CHARYBDIS [kuh RIB dis], a monster who engulfed anyone and anything that came near her. Charybdis was in the form of a whirlpool between the "toe" of Italy and the island Sicily. Odysseus passed Charybdis twice on his homeward voyage. He had a narrow escape the second time, but through Athene's efforts, his life was spared.

CIRCE [SUR see], the beautiful witch who transformed six of Odysseus' men into swine. Odysseus outwitted her and remained on her island for one year. Circe was the daughter of Helios.

CYCLOPES [seye KLOH peez], the plural of *Cyclops* [SEYE klops], a race of monster-giants who looked like men. They were as strong and violent as hurricanes, volcanoes, and earth-quakes. *Cyclops* means "round-eye" and describes the enormous eye in the middle of the Cyclops' forehead. [*See* Polyphemus.]

DEMODOCUS [duh MOD uh kus], a blind minstrel, was bard to the court of Alcinous. In ancient Greece these highly respected minstrels sang stories of gods and of heroes in war. Many bards had the gift of prophecy and followed the armies to war. In an age when most people could neither read nor write, they acted as on-the-scene reporters. Since their tales and stories were sung, these prophet-bards were skilled in the arts of verse and music. The poet Homer was a wandering minstrel, whose *Iliad* and *Odyssey* are myths about the Trojan War and the voyage of Odysseus.

EREBUS [ER uh bus], the "dark realm beneath the Earth"—the part of the Underworld to which the Greeks believed people went after they died. [*See* Tartarus.]

EUMAEUS [yoo MEE us], son of the king of Syria. As a child, Eumaeus was taken to Phaeacia by one of his father's bond maids. On the way, the bond maid was shot by Artemis and drowned. Angry Zeus unleashed winds and caused Eumaeus and the ship's crew to be cast ashore on the island of Ithaca. Laertes bought the boy and reared him as his own son. When the boy grew up, he became Odysseus' swineherd and faithfully watched over the interests of Odysseus until his master returned from the war.

EURYCLEIA [yoor uh KLEE uh], the shrewd nurse who cared for Odysseus from the day he was born. She brought the infant to his grandfather saying to him, "Here is your daughter's son. Invent a suitable name for him." The grandfather named him Odysseus—"odiousness"—to stand for all the complaints of mankind. When, after twenty years absence, Odysseus returned dressed as a beggar, Eurycleia recognized her master.

EURYLOCHUS [yoo RIL uh kus], the second in command of Odysseus' fleet. He was married to Odysseus' sister.

EURYMACHUS [yoo RIM uh kus], son of a wise father, was more than a mortal being to the Ithacans. Among those who were Penelope's suitors, he showed greater promise than the others.

HADES [HAY deez], brother of Zeus, and ruler of the Underworld. Hades is also the name of the dismal underworld land of the dead. The Greek word *hades* means "invisible." People in the Underworld did not change much in appearance, but they took on a shadowy likeness of their earthly forms. They acted and looked very much like ghosts but they continued their human habits of eating, drinking, and speaking. Odysseus was the only mortal who ever entered the Underworld and lived to tell about the horrible experience.

HELIOS [HEE lee os], God of the Sun. He drove a chariot daily across the sky. Helios kept his sacred cattle on Threnacia—the present-day island of Sicily. Odysseus' men feasted on Helios' herds while they stayed on Threnacia.

HERMES [HUR meez], son of Zeus, and messenger of the gods. Hermes was sent from Mount Olympus to Calypso's island of Ogygia with the command from Zeus to release Odysseus. The young and handsome god gave Odysseus some sound advice. And he gave Odysseus the moly plant that helped to overcome Circe's magic spell. Hermes was the most popular god on Mount Olympus and appears more often in the Greek myths than any other god. He was noted for his cunning, his pranks, and his inventiveness.

INO [EYE noh], daughter-in-law of Aeolus. Hera, the wife of Zeus, afflicted Ino and her husband with madness. Poseidon took pity on Ino and transformed her into a sea goddess.

ISMARUS [ISS mur us], city of the Cicones, where Odysseus lost seventy-two of his men.

ITHACA [ITH uh kuh], an island in the Ionian Sea, and the kingdom of Odysseus.

LAESTRYGONES [les TRIG uh neez], giant cannibals descended from the god Poseidon. They destroyed eleven of Odysseus' ships and their crews.

LAMOS [LAH mos], a fortress given the name "tall-tower" by the Laestrygones.

MENELAUS [men uh LAY us], king of Sparta, and brother of Agamemnon. Menelaus' wife, Helen, known for her beauty, was persuaded by Paris to elope with him to Troy. Menelaus organized the Greek army for an attack on Troy to recover his wife. In order that Telemachus could learn news of his father, Athene sent him to Menelaus.

MINOS [MY nos], son of Zeus, and mythical king of Crete. He was renowned for justice and wisdom, and became a judge of the dead in Hades. Odysseus met Minos when he visited the Underworld.

NAUSICAA [naw SIK ee uh], daughter of Alcinous, king of the Phaeacians. Athene charmed her in order that she would be on the beach, prepared with clothes and food to rescue the shipwrecked Odysseus.

ODYSSEUS [oh DIS ee us], one of the most popular figures in ancient Greek literature. A wise, resourceful, and courageous king, he was godlike and not entirely a legendary person. The myths and stories that have been told over and over again are believed to be based on an actual hero of early Greek times.

OGYGIA [oh JIJ ee uh], the remote and idyllic island that Odysseus reached after his ship and crew were lost at sea.

ORION [oh RYE un], a descendent of Poseidon, was a hunter of gigantic size and great beauty. After his death, he lived in the Underworld and appeared in the heavens as a constellation—complete with sword, club, and lion's skin. Odysseus saw Orion when he visited the Underworld.

PENELOPE [puh NEL uh pee], the loyal wife of Odysseus. She refused to believe reports that he was dead, and put off her numerous suitors with a clever trick. She promised to choose a new husband when she finished weaving a funeral shroud for Laertes, father of Odysseus. For three years she worked on the shroud by day and unraveled it at night.

PERSEPHONE [pur SEF uh nee], daughter of Zeus, and wife of Hades. She spent four months of each year in the Underworld. During this time, the Earth lay barren and lifeless. But when she returned to Earth, it blossomed into spring and for eight months the Earth enjoyed the life-giving seasons. She is known as the Maid of Spring.

POLYPHEMUS [pol uh FEE mus], a Cyclops and son of Poseidon. He was a shepherd and a forger of armor, the two occupations practiced by the Cyclopes. Poseidon was so enraged at Odysseus and his men for blinding Polyphemus that he made their voyage to Ithaca a nightmare.

POSEIDON [puh SEYE dun], brother of Zeus, and ruler of the oceans. He was the arch-enemy of Odysseus. Because of Poseidon's untiring wrath, the voyage of Odysseus was marked by great suffering and disaster.

SCYLLA [SIL uh], a monster that preyed upon ships that passed through the narrow strait below her cave. She had twelve feet, and the body of a woman from the waist up. Each of her six heads had three rows of teeth encrusted with human blood. Scylla snatched six of Odysseus' men from the ship in one dreadful swoop. Her cave was opposite Charybdis.

SIRENS [SEYE runz], women with enchanting voices who lived on an island in the sea. No one knew what they looked like. If Odysseus had not been warned by Circe, he and his men would have met instant death after being lured to the Sirens' island by their singing and by promises of great knowledge.

TARTARUS [TAHR tuhr us], a prison deep under the Earth, where evil men and gods were sent to be punished. For this reason, Tartarus is associated with great suffering. Tartarus and Erebus were both divisions of the Underworld, and covered the entire area under the earth.

TELEMACHUS [tuh LEM uh kus], son of Odysseus and Penelope, was an infant when his father left for Troy. When Odysseus returned twenty years later, Telemachus helped him slay Penelope's suitors.

TIRESIAS [tye REE see us], a blind prophet of Thebes who counseled Odysseus on his voyage and his return to Ithaca. Circe had advised Odysseus to go to the Underworld to seek out the ghost of Tiresias and learn from him what to expect of the future.

TROY, a city, now called Hissarlik, in northwest Asia Minor at the entrance to the Dardanelles. The ancient city of Troy was ruled by Priam and was sacked by the Greek army under the leadership of Agamemnon. Homer's epic poem, the *Iliad*, is an account of this war.

ZEUS [ZOOS], father of the gods on Mount Olympus. He was an ally of the Greeks in the legendary account of the Trojan War. After the war, Athene and Poseidon persuaded him to use his power against the Greeks. Zeus and his brother Poseidon joined forces against Odysseus. Athene took pity on Odysseus, and at her request, Zeus commanded Calypso to release Odysseus from her island.